Muhammad Ali

JULIA HOLT

GW00703268

ALBSU *The Basic Skills Unit*

Registered Charity № 1005969

There is a man
who has two different names.
He is world famous
with both of them.

He floats like a butterfly,
stings like a bee,
he is the greatest,
Muhammad Ali.

Early Days

One day in 1954,
at the age of 12,
Cassius Clay went into town
on his bike.

His bike was stolen
and he went to a nearby gym
to get help.

He saw men boxing
and he became interested.

Clay started to train.

He worked very hard.
After 6 weeks
he won his first fight.

He became so good
that he boxed
in the 1960 Rome Olympics.

Clay won a gold medal.

Clay knew
he could make a living
out of boxing.

He could make the money
he needed for his family.

So he became a showman,
a professional boxer
with very fast feet,
and a big mouth.

He said "I am the greatest".

In 1963
Clay came to England
to fight Henry Cooper.

He came into the ring
in a red coat
and a golden crown.

He said he would win
in round 5,
and he did.

But not before
Cooper knocked him down
in the 4th round,
just before the bell.

Heavy-weight Champion

Clay wanted to try to win
the world title.

So in 1964
he fought Sonny Liston.

Liston was a boxer
to be feared.

He had been in prison
for armed robbery.

This did not stop Clay
from calling him
a big ugly bear.

At the end of round 6,
Liston stopped fighting.
He said he was hurt.

Clay became
heavy-weight champion
of the world.

But some people said
the fight was a fix.

After this fight,
Clay told the newspapers
that he was a Muslim.

He became Muhammad Ali,
because his old name
was a slave's name.

Black Muslims were not popular
in America,
because they said
white people were the enemy.

After this,
Ali was not so popular
with some people.

In 1964,
Ali married
the first of his four wives.

They were divorced
after 2 years.

Then Ali fought Liston again.
This time he knocked Liston out
after only 60 seconds.

It was a short blow to the chin.
It was so fast, no-one saw it,
so they said
it was a fix again.

Ali was told he had to join the army
to fight in Vietnam.

He said he was a Muslim,
and he would not go to war.

For this,
he was fined 10,000 dollars,
and his world title
was taken away.

For the next three years,
he was not allowed to box.

This was a big blow to him,
but he went on with his life.

He married
17 year-old Belinda
and they had 4 children.

Heavy-weight Champion Again!

When he came back to boxing,
he was slower than before.

Because he was slower
he got hit badly
for the first time.

He lost fights
to Frazier, Patterson and Norton.

Ken Norton broke Ali's jaw.

People said he was finished
but he was not.

He fought them all again,
and won.

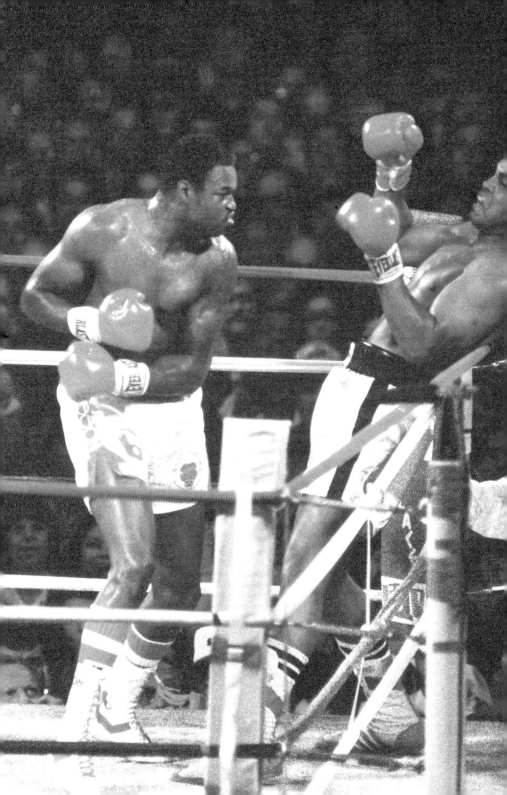

Next he wanted
his title back.

He had to fight George Forman
in Africa in 1974.

This was the famous
rumble in the jungle.

Before the fight,
Ali said:

"I float like a butterfly,
Sting like a bee,
His hands can't hit
What his eyes can't see!"

He won the fight
by a knock-out.

Seven years after
his title was taken away,
he had got it back.

He was 32 years old.

Ali lost his title again
for one year,
to Leon Spinks.

He got it back
and kept it
until he stopped boxing
in 1979.

Ali's career lasted 20 years.
He had 56 wins
with 37 knock-outs.

He lost only 5 times.

Ali married his third wife
in 1977.
They had 2 children.

Now he lives on a farm
with Lonnie,
his fourth wife.

Sadly, he has brain damage,
because he was hit
on the head
so many times
in his boxing days.

But he is still loved and respected.
He will always be the greatest.

He still travels the world.
He still signs 2,000 autographs a week.

And he still wants to know
who stole his bike
back in 1954!